Expository Outlines from Romans

Croft M. Pentz

Baker Book House
Grand Rapids, Michigan

Copyright 1980 by
Baker Book House Company
ISBN: 0-8010-7057-0

Fourth printing, November 1985

Scripture quotations are from the King James Version unless marked otherwise. Other versions quoted are: The Living Bible (LB) and The New Life Testament (NLT).

PHOTOLITHOPRINTED BY CUSHING - MALLOY, INC.
ANN ARBOR, MICHIGAN, UNITED STATES OF AMERICA

Contents

1 The Gospel of Jesus Christ (1:1-17)............... 4
2 Rejecting the Gospel (1:18-32)................ 5
3 Judgment for All (2:1-16)................. 7
4 Salvation or the Law? (2:17-29)............... 8
5 Self-righteous People (3:1-18)............. 10
6 Redeemed by the Law (3:19-31)............ 11
7 Righteous Through Faith (4:1-25............ 13
8 Salvation Through Christ (5:1-11)............ 15
9 Sin and Salvation (5:12-21)............. 17
10 Freedom from Sin (6:1-14)............ 18
11 The Power of Choice (6:15-23)............ 20
12 The Weakness of the Law (7:1-13)............ 21
13 Servants of God or Sin (7:14-25)............ 23
14 The Power of the Spirit (8:1-19)............ 24
15 The Assurance of Salvation (8:20-34)............ 26
16 Untouchable in Christ (8:35-39)............ 27
17 The Plan of God (9:1-18)............ 29
18 Acceptance or Rejection (9:19-33)............ 31
19 The Plan of Salvation (10:1-21)............ 32
20 God's Love for the Jews (11:1-24)............ 34
21 The All-powerful God of Salvation (11:25-36)............ 35
22 The Serving Christian (12:1-8)............ 37
23 The Mature Christian (12:9-21)............ 38
24 Christian Righteousness (13:1-14)............ 40
25 Christian Consideration (14:1-23)............ 42
26 Responsible to God's Will (15:1-21)............ 44
27 Concern and Care (15:22-33)............ 45
28 Fellowship and Farewell (16:1-27)............ 47

1 The Gospel of Jesus Christ

Romans 1:1-17

The gospel is the good news of salvation. It is first mentioned in Matthew 4:23: "Jesus went about—preaching the gospel." It is last mentioned in Revelation 14:6. Power in the gospel to save, keep, heal and satisfy is ours for simply believing.

A. The People and the Gospel—vv. 1-7
1. The Servant—v. 1. Paul was called to be an apostle for the preaching of the gospel—Acts 9:1-6.
2. The Scriptures—v. 2. God promised the gospel through the prophets—Luke 24:44; Heb. 1:1.
3. The Son—vv. 3-6
   a) Incarnation—v. 3 The Word became flesh—John 1:14; Phil. 2:5-8.
   b) Infallible—v. 4. The perfect Son of God—Col. 2:9. In Him dwells the power of God.
   c) Impact—vv. 5-6. When converted, we are commanded to share the good news—Mark 15:16.
4. The saints—v. 7. To all the saints at Rome, grace and peace. Note: "called to be saints." See I Peter 5:10, the call of God.

B. The Preaching of the Gospel—vv. 8-15
1. Pleasure—v. 8. Paul was pleased with the renowned faith of the Roman Christians. This dedication spreads to others—Rom. 16:19.
2. Prayer—vv. 9-10. Paul prayed for their needs and for an opportunity to visit them. Note Jesus' prayer for the church—John 17:20.
3. Plea—vv. 11-12. He wanted to impart spiritual blessings, to establish and encourage them in the Lord. Cf. Matt. 5:48.
4. Preaching—v. 15. Paul was ready to preach the gospel. Cf. Jer. 20:9.

C. The Power of the Gospel—vv. 16-17
1. Gospel of power—v. 16. It is the basis for salvation and

4

transformation—Heb. 4:12; for all who believe—Rom. 10:13; first for the Jew, then for the Gentile (Whosoever!).
2. Gospel of pardon—v. 17. (See also Hab. 2:4.) "The man who finds life will find it through trusting God"—LB. We are saved by faith—Eph. 2:8–9.

After we experience the power of the gospel, we should share it. We are commanded as Christians to go into all the world and preach the gospel—Mark 16:15. If we are ashamed of our gospel, we will hide it from those who are lost—II Cor. 4:3. Paul was not ashamed of the gospel of Christ—v. 16. Note the results of being ashamed of Jesus—Mark 8:38.

2 Rejecting the Gospel

Romans 1:18–32

God has given man freedom of choice. See also Josh. 24:15; I Kings 18:21. God doesn't force anyone to follow His way. Our life now as well as in eternity depends on our acceptance or rejection of the gospel. No one can choose for us; every person is responsible to God for his own choices.

A. **Stubbornness toward God—vv. 18–23**
1. Revelation—vv. 18–19. God's wrath is revealed against ungodliness and unrighteousness. He demands holiness—Heb. 12:14.
2. Reality—v. 20. Man has seen nature, evidence of God who created and controls it. He says in his heart, there is no God—Ps. 14:1.
3. Rejection—v. 21. "They did know God, but they did not honor Him as God. They were not thankful to Him and thought only of foolish things. Their foolish minds became dark"—NLT. Men love darkness—John 3:19.
4. Reaction—vv. 22–23. Thinking they were wise, they became fools. Note: "Fools make a mock of sin"—Prov. 14:9.

B. Separation from God — vv. 24–27
1. Denounced — v. 24. God gave them up because of their corruption. Our sin separates us from God — Isa. 59:2.
2. Depravity — v. 25. They worshiped the creature more than the Creator. God forbids idol worship — Exod. 20:4. See also I John 5:21. Our idols could be money, sleep, friends, family, etc.
3. Degradation — vv. 26–27. Homosexuality is not a sickness — it is sin! God destroyed Sodom and Gomorrah because of this sin — Gen. 19:1–26. See also Lev. 18:22; Deut. 23:17–18; I Cor. 6:19–20.

C. Sinfulness against God — vv. 28–32
1. Sorrow — v. 28. God gave up these people who rebelled against Him. If we believe, we are saved; if we do not believe, we are lost — Mark 16:16; John 3:18.
2. Sins — vv. 29–31. "Their lives became full of every kind of wickedness and sin, of greed and hate, envy, murder, fighting, lying, bitterness, and gossip. They were backbiters, haters of God, insolent, proud braggarts, always thinking of new ways of sinning and continually being disobedient to their parents. They tried to misunderstand, broke their promises, and were heartless — without pity" — LB.
3. Shame — v. 32. They enjoyed sinning and getting others to sin. See Isa. 5:20: evil is called good.

What a shame! Knowing what is right, but rejecting it; rejecting also an opportunity to have sins forgiven, to have everlasting life. Satan hardens man's heart — II Cor. 4:4. As man continues to reject God, his heart becomes hardened; he feels no conviction. The Spirit can quicken this heart and life — Eph. 2:1.

3 Judgment for All

Romans 2:1-16

There is only one righteous judge—God. Regardless of one's experience, skill or intelligence, no one is qualified to judge another. Jesus warned against judging—Matt. 7:1-5. If we heed Paul's advice in I Corinthians 9:24-27, we will have no time to judge others. Judging others shows a lack of consecration and maturity.

A. The Sin of Judging—vv. 1-4
1. The judging—v. 1. When we judge others, we are judging ourselves. We may not have the sins of Romans 1:21-32, but that does not mean we should become self-righteous and proud. We are all sinners—Rom. 3:23.
2. The judge—v. 2. God is the righteous judge—Ps. 103:6. Let Him do the judging.
3. The judgment—v. 3. "Do you think that God will judge and condemn others for doing them (committing the aforementioned sins) and overlook you when you do them too?"—LB. All Christians will be judged—II Cor. 5:10.
4. The justice—v. 4. God's kindness and patience lead us to repentance and new life in Christ. See II Peter 3:9. God desires that all turn from their sins, that none be lost.

B. The Self in Judging—vv. 5-11
1. Righteous judgment—vv. 5-6. Stubbornness in continuing to sin adds to the wrath the sinner will face in God's final judgment—Rev. 20:11-15. We are judged by the heart (v. 5); judged by our deeds (v. 6). See also Mal. 3:16. God keeps a record of all who love Him.
2. Results in judgment—vv. 7-8.
   a) Righteous—v. 7. Eternal life. Our name must be in the Lamb's Book of Life—Rev. 21:27; 20:15.
   b) Rebellion—v. 8. "Those who love only themselves and do not obey the truth, but do what is wrong, will be punished by God. His anger will be on them"—NLT.

3. Reasoning in judgment — vv. 9–11. Jew and Gentile, all must stand before God. He is no respecter of persons — Rom. 10:12. The gospel of salvation is for all people — Rom. 1:16.

C. **The Savior in Judging — vv. 12–16**
   1. Judgment on all men — vv. 12–15. We are sinners — Isa. 53:6. All sin must be punished — Rom. 6:23. The "small and great" shall stand before God — Rev. 20:11–15. If man sincerely seeks God, he will find God — Jer. 29:13.
   2. Judgment on all motives — v. 16. All must die, then comes judgment — Heb. 9:27. We will be judged by the use of our abilities — Luke 12:48. We will be rewarded according to our works — Rev. 22:12. What we sow, we will reap — Gal. 6:7, 8.

God will judge all sin, whether in the life of a sinner or a Christian who has become cold. If the sin is not confessed and forsaken, God's judgment will fall on that person. It will mean separation from God. Paul advises us to examine ourselves — I Cor. 11:28.

4 Salvation or the Law?

Romans 2:17–29

The Jews were very strict in keeping their ceremonial laws. They had a form of religion but lacked faith in God. They were faithful to their teachings but were not forgiven of their sins. They were religious but lost.

A. **Spiritual Pride — vv. 17–20**
   1. Pride — vv. 17–18. Because God gave them the law (the Ten Commandments and other Laws), the Jews thought they were righteous. Cf. Rom. 3:23.
   2. Practice — v. 19. They thought they had the truth and could teach others. They rejected Christ, who *was* the truth — John 14:6; 16:13. How could they guide others into truth they didn't have?

3. Plan — v. 20. How could they teach others when they themselves were in darkness? Jesus spoke of the blind leading the blind — Matt. 15:14. An unconverted religious leader cannot lead others to righteous living.

B. Spiritual Practice — vv. 21-24
If you teach others, do you practice what you teach? Paul warns of people having a form of godliness, but no power or reality of the gospel — II Tim. 3:1-5.
1. The practice — vv. 21-22. "Yes, you teach others — then why don't you teach yourselves? You tell others not to steal — do *you* steal? You say it is wrong to commit adultery — do *you* do it? You say, 'Don't pray to idols,' and then make money your god instead" — LB. They said they knew God, but their works denied it — Titus 1:16.
2. The problem — v. 23. They knew the Old Testament teachings, but they didn't obey them. See also Matt. 7:21-23; Rev. 3:17-18.
3. The pity — v. 24. Because of the poor example of professed Christians, the name of Christ is often treated with disrespect — Luke 6:46; John 14:15.

C. Spiritual Purity — vv. 25-29
1. Religious or righteous? — vv. 25-26. Practicing a religious act will not make us right with God. The rich ruler obeyed laws but was not a Christian — Mark 10:17-22.
2. Sacrilegious or sacred — vv. 27-28. Jewish laws did not measure up to God's laws. Note Eph. 2:8-9. It is not what we do but what Christ has done for us that atones for our sins.
3. Historical or holy — v. 29. God is not looking for a historical religion, but for holy (set apart) people who love and serve Him. See Heb. 12:14. Only the pure in heart will see God — Matt. 5:8. We must be born again — John 3:18.

There are many religious people who will not go to heaven. Only Christ through the new birth can make us righteous — John 3:1-8; II Cor. 5:17. His blood will cleanse us from all sin — I John 1:7. He will forgive all sins — Ps. 103:3. If we confess our sins, He will forgive — I John 1:9. We will be assured of eternal life. The Jewish law couldn't promise this.

5 Self-righteous People

Romans 3:1–18

The Jews were self-righteous people. They depended on the Jewish ceremonial laws for salvation. From Ephesians 2:8–9 we learn that even today many pin their hopes for salvation on the works that they do rather than on what God has done for them.

A. The Pride of These People — vv. 1–4
1. Pride — v. 1. Are the Jews better in the sight of God than the non-Jews? See Matt. 6:2, 16. All are equal in His sight.
2. Provision — v. 2. The Jews were the first to receive the gospel of salvation — Rom. 1:16. This does not mean God loves the Jew more than the Gentile.
3. Problem — v. 3. Because the Jews were unfaithful does not mean God isn't faithful — I Cor. 10:13.
4. Personality — v. 4. God is truthful even when all others are not. Christ is the truth — John 14:6. God does not lie — Titus 1:2; Num. 23:19.

B. The Problem of These People — vv. 5–8
1. Folly — v. 5. "If our sins show how right God is, what can we say? It is wrong for God to punish us for it? (I am speaking as men do)" — NLT. He is righteous in all ways — Ps. 145:17.
2. Fairness — v. 6. He will judge in a fair manner — Rev. 20:11–15 ("The books were opened.") Note also God's book of remembrance — Mal. 3:16. No excuses will be accepted, no exceptions given. He will have the evidence.
3. Foolishness — vv. 7–8. "If my lies honor God by showing how true He is, why am I still being punished as a sinner? Why not say, 'Let us sin that good will come from it.' (Some people have said I talk like this.) They will be punished as they should be" — NLT. If we call ourselves Christians, we should depart from all sin — II Tim. 2:19.

C. The Personality of These People — vv. 9–18
1. Sin — vv. 9–10. Both Jew and Gentile are sinners — Rom. 3:23; Isa. 53:6; Ps. 51:5.

2. Slothful — v. 11. No one understands or seeks God. God looked down from heaven to see if any sought God — Ps. 14:2.
3. Stubborn — v. 12. They chose to go astray. "The heart is deceitful above all things, and desperately wicked" — Jer. 17:9.
4. Shame — vv. 12-18. Unprofitable people:
   a) Throat — v. 13. Deceit. Cf. James 3:6.
   b) Mouth — v. 14. Cursing and bitterness — I Peter 2:1.
   c) Feet — v. 15. Shed blood — Prov. 6:18.
   d) Ways — v. 16. Destruction and misery — Prov. 2:15.
   e) No respect — vv. 17-18. No peace or honor — Isa. 48:22.

The Pharisees had a form of religion but didn't know God in a personal way. They fasted, prayed, paid tithes, but these were outward manifestations only. They did not have God in their hearts — Matt. 7:24-27. Religion and deeds will not save man. He must be born again — John 3:3.

6 Redeemed by the Law

Romans 3:19-31

Keeping the Old Testament laws, including the Ten Commandments, will not save. When man is born again, he will keep the Ten Commandments. The Old Testament law was "an eye for an eye and a tooth for a tooth." Christ's command was completely different — Matt. 5:43-44. Note: "But I say unto you."

A. Responsibility — vv. 19-20
1. Responsible — v. 19. The Jews had the laws of God. They were responsible to God. See John 7:17. If you seek God, He will reveal His will. If we seek Him, we will find Him — Jer. 29:13.
2. Revelation — v. 20. The Old Testament revealed man's sin. See the Ten Commandments (Exod. 20:1-7).

11

B. Righteousness — vv. 21–24
1. Pardon — v. 21. God's way of salvation and righteousness is through Christ. See John 14:6; Acts 4:12.
2. Plan — v. 22. Righteousness by faith is for all who believe. Being born again (John 3:1–8) makes us the sons of God — John 1:12; I John 3:2, 3.
3. Problem — v. 23. All are sinners — Rom. 3:10. Everyone has gone astray — Isa. 53:6.
4. Perfection — v. 24. Justified! By His grace, we are righteous before God through Christ. Redeemed from sin — I Cor. 1:30.

C. Remission — vv. 25–26
1. The plan — v. 25. "For God sent Christ Jesus to take the punishment for our sins and to end all God's anger against us. He used Christ's blood and our faith as the means of saving us from His wrath. In this He was being entirely fair, even though He did not punish those who sinned in former times. For He was looking forward to the time when Christ would come and take away those sins" — LB.
2. The pardon — v. 26. He forgives all sin. He saves to the uttermost — Heb. 7:25. All who call upon Him will be saved — Rom. 10:13, John 6:37.

D. Relationship — vv. 27–31
1. Conversion — vv. 27–28. Our salvation is not based on what the law has done but on what Christ has done. We are saved by faith — Rom. 5:1; Gal. 3:24.
2. Comparison — vv. 29–30. Jew or Greek — all are sinners. All may be saved — Rom. 1:16. God loved the world — John 3:16.
3. Control — v. 31. Do we obey the Ten Commandments? Of course we do! James 1:25 speaks of the perfect law of God.

If the law would have saved, why did Christ suffer and die on the cross? We are saved by grace — Acts 15:11. When the Philippian jailer asked Paul what he had to do to be saved, the answer was simple, "Believe on the Lord Jesus Christ" — Acts 16:30–31.

7 Righteous Through Faith

Romans 4:1-25

Abraham was accounted righteous by his faith—not good works. Our righteousness is as filthy rags—Isa. 64:6. We are righteous only through the new birth—John 3:1-8; II Cor. 5:17. To be right with God, we must be right with our fellowman. Note Abraham's faith—Heb. 11:8-12.

A. Righteous Through Faith—vv. 1-12
1. Person—vv. 1-2. "Abraham was, humanly speaking, the founder of our Jewish nation. What were his experiences concerning this question of being saved by faith? Was it because of his good deeds that God accepted him? If so, then he would have something to boast about. But from God's point of view Abraham had no basis at all for pride"—LB.
2. Pardon—v. 3. Faith counted to Abraham for righteousness.
3. Plan—vv. 4-5. God counts us righteous, not for our good works but for our faith. Sinners will be made saints—I John 3:2.
4. Peace—vv. 6-8. Peace comes through having our sins forgiven—Ps. 32:1-2.
5. Plan—vv. 9-12
   a) Formality—vv. 9-10. Abraham was not saved by forms of law. God blessed Abraham before he was circumcised.
   b) Faith—vv. 11-12. Abraham found favor with God by faith alone.

B. Righteous Through Fellowship—vv. 13-15
1. Promise—v. 13. God promised Abraham blessings because he believed God and obeyed. See John 14:15.
2. Problem—v. 14. "If those who obey the Jewish law are to get the world, then a person putting his trust in God means nothing. God's promise to Abraham would be worth nothing"—NLT.

3. Plan—v. 15. God's anger falls on those who break the law. If we break one part of the law, we are guilty of breaking the whole law—James 2:10.

C. Righteous Through Following—vv. 16-25
1. Plan—v. 16. All God's blessings come by faith—not the law. See Heb. 11:6.
2. People—v. 17. Abraham was the father of the Jewish nation. (Gen. 17:4-5). As God gave new life to Isaac, so He gives new life to us—John 10:10.
3. Problem—vv. 18-22
   a) Age—vv. 18-19. Abraham was one hundred and Sarah ninety; yet God gave them a son. See Matt. 19:26.
   b) Answer—vv. 21-22. Abraham had complete faith in God.
4. Promise—vv. 23-24. Quotation from Gen. 15:6. As God accepted Abraham, so He accepts us. See John 1:12.
5. Pardon—v. 25. Through Christ we are saved. Rom. 10:9-10.

After we accept Christ as Saviour, we must maintain our relationship with the Lord. Paul spoke of cleansing ourselves from sin—I Cor. 6:11; 7:1. We must seek to live a pure and holy life—Heb. 12:14; Rev. 21:27.

8 Salvation Through Christ

Romans 5:1-11

In Paul's writings, two prominent words are *faith* and *believe*. These two words are more than mental assent. Later Paul spoke of believing in God with the heart — Rom. 10:9-10. This is the kind of belief that is necessary for salvation.

A. Peace with God — vv. 1-2
1. Accepted by faith — v. 1. To be justified is to be made right with God. The word *justification* means "just as if I didn't sin" — forgiven and the sin forgotten. Faith is necessary for peace with God:
   a) Plan of peace — Isa. 53:5
   b) Provision of peace — Col. 1:20
   c) Person bringing peace — Eph. 2:14
2. Access by faith — v. 2
   a) Plan of access — Ps. 24:3-4
   b) Provision for access — John 10:9
   c) Powerful access — Eph. 3:12
Because we belong to God's family, we rejoice, having hope of eternal glory, eternal life — John 5:24.

B. Patience with God — vv. 3-5
1. Reason for problems — v. 3. We glory in tribulation. This will bring us patience.
   a) Persecution — Matt. 5:10-12: blessed by God.
   b) Punishment — Acts 5:41: rejoicing to be counted worthy to suffer for Christ.
   c) Plan — Job 23:10: when tested, to come forth as gold.
   d) Purpose — Ps. 119:67: straying before afflicted.
   e) Patience — Rom. 8:28: all things for a reason or purpose.
2. Results of problems — v. 4. Patience brings two things: experience — the ability to deal with a problem; hope — knowing the problem is for our good.

3. Reassurance in problems—v. 5. "Hope never makes us ashamed because the love of God has come into our hearts through the Holy Spirit Who was given to us"—NLT. Note the hope we have—I John 3:2-3.

C. Pardon by God—vv. 6-11
1. Weak—v. 6. Sinful man was without strength, hopeless, doomed. Rom. 3:23; 6:23. Christ took our hell on the cross—I Peter 3:18. He suffered to bring us to God.
2. Willingness—v. 7. Who would die for an enemy? Christ did! He took our place, because of our sin—Isa. 53:5-6; John 3:16; 15:5-6.
3. Wonder—v. 8. What great love! See Jer. 31:3.
4. Work—vv. 9-11
    a) Redeemed—v. 9. Free from the judgment of Revelation 20:11-15.
    b) Reconciled—v. 10. Separated by sin, now reconciled through Christ.
    c) Rejoicing—v. 11. "In thy presence is fulness of joy"—Ps. 16:11.

Salvation brings responsibility with each blessing. Jesus tells us (Luke 9:23) that we must bear our cross daily. This involves various forms of suffering, persecution, pain and problems, but Christ stands with us through all of these. The joy and benefits far outweigh the problems.

9 Sin and Salvation

Romans 5:12-21

God created Adam and Eve perfect, to live forever. Sin marred this perfection for all mankind. (See Ps. 51:5; Rom. 6:10.) Man's heart is naturally evil—Jer. 17:9. Christ came to redeem man from his sin; only in Christ can he be made new—II Cor. 5:17. He will be given a new heart—Ezek. 36:26.

A. The Start of Sin—vv. 12-14
1. Start—v. 12
   a) Degradation—v. 12a. Sin came through Adam's sin— Gen. 3:1-15.
   b) Death—v. 12b. Death came to all—Rom. 6:23; Ezek. 18:20.
2. Sin—v. 13. "Sin was in the world before the Jewish Law was given. But sin is not held against a person when there is no law"—NLT.
3. Separation—v. 14. Sin brings death—Gen. 2:17. "If you eat of this tree you will die." Sin always separates us from God (Ps. 66:18).

B. The Stigma of Sin—vv. 15-19
1. Security—v. 15. "God's free gift is not like the sin of Adam. Many people died because of the sin of this one man, Adam. But the loving favor of God came to many people also. This gift came also by one man, Jesus Christ, God's Son"—NLT.
2. Salvation—v. 16. "The free gift of God is not like Adam's sin. God told Adam he was guilty because of his sin and guilt. But the free gift makes men right with God. Through One, Christ, men's sins are forgiven"—NLT.
3. Sin—v. 17. Because of man's sin, death reigned; all are born in sin—Rom. 3:23. Note the results of sin—Rev. 21:8.
4. Saviour—v. 18. Through Adam all are sinners. Christ's righteousness is imputed to those who are His. We must be born again—John 3:1-8.

17

5. Surrender—v. 19. Surrender to Christ and God's will. His plan gives us all righteousness. See Phil. 2:5-11. Adam's disobedience made us sinners. Christ's obedience clothes those who are His with His righteousness.

C. The Salvation from Sin—vv. 20-21

1. Power of sin—v. 20. "Sin spread when the Jewish Law was given. But where sin spread, God's loving-favor spread all the more"—NLT. When sin grew, God's grace abounded more and more. Note Eph. 1:7. Through His grace we have redemption.
2. Power of salvation—v. 21. Sin meant death. Christ's death meant life. Note the choice—Rom. 6:23. The wages of sin is death, but God's gift is everlasting life. In Him was life—John 1:4; abundant life—John 10:10; eternal life—John 3:16; 11:25-26.

Though sin may abound, and though Satan may be powerful, God is over all. When He lives in us, we are more powerful than sin or Satan (I John 4:4). When Christ, the Truth (John 14:6), is in us, this truth will set us free (John 8:32). As God's children, we remain free.

10 Freedom from Sin

Romans 6:1-14

Sin always brings bondage—of the body, mind, soul and will. Sin enslaves us (John 8:34) to its problems and practices. Christ came to set us free from this slavery!

A. Salvation from Sin—vv. 1-5

1. Reasoning—v. 1. Should we continue in sin so we may have more of God's grace? See II Tim. 2:19. Newness of life in Christ—II Cor. 5:17.

18

2. Rejection — v. 2. When in Christ, we no longer live in sin but have crucified the flesh, the affections and lust — Gal. 5:24; Gal. 2:20.
3. Relations — v. 3. Those in Christ must share in His death. Jesus spoke of self-denial — Luke 9:23. A Christian life is surrendered to God, not patterned after this world — Rom. 12:1-2.
4. Results — vv. 4-5. We are buried with the Lord in baptism, and raised with Him. Baptism is symbolic of inner cleansing, burying our sin, then rising to walk in newness of life in the Spirit — Gal. 5:16. We are to walk by faith, not by sight — II Cor. 5:7.

B. Separation from Sin — vv. 6-11
1. Denial — v. 6. The "old man" is crucified. By birth, we were the children of Satan — John 8:44. In Christ we are the children of God — John 1:12.
2. Death — v. 7. Dead to sin, we are freed; no longer a servant of sin — John 8:34; no longer do we sin by choice and habit — John 8:32, 36.
3. Dominion — vv. 8-9. Death had dominion over us (I Cor. 15:51-58), but Christ conquered death for us. See John 11:25-26.
4. Design — vv. 10-11. "He died once but now lives. He died to break the power of sin, and the life He now lives is for God. You must do the same thing! Think of yourselves as dead to the power of sin. But now you have new life because of Jesus Christ our Lord. You are living this new life for God" — NLT.

C. Sanctification from Sin — vv. 12-14
1. Denounced — v. 12. Don't allow sin with its lusts to rule you — Dan. 1:8; James 1:14-15. Lust brings separation from God.
2. Dedication — v. 13. Don't yield your body to sin, but to God. See Ps. 119:9, 11.
3. Dominion — v. 14. Sin doesn't have to control you. We are not under the law — Rom. 8:2; II Cor. 3:17.

Salvation brings freedom from sin. Some return to the old ways of sin. Heed Paul's advice—Gal. 5:1. We need not be bound by any sin; there is power to overcome every temptation—I Cor. 10:13.

11 The Power of Choice

Romans 6:15-23

God made man a free moral agent. Adam and Eve chose to disobey God. Joshua admonished, "Choose you this day whom ye will serve"— Josh. 24:15. Elijah also demanded a decision—I Kings 18:21. Christ came to His own and they chose to reject Him—John 1:11. If we believe, we will be saved; if we reject Christ, we will be lost—Mark 16:16. Man's eternal destiny is dependent on his choice.

A. The Choice of Slavery—vv. 15-19
1. Choice—v. 15. If we yield to sin, we are servants to sin—John 8:34; if to Christ, then sons of God—John 1:12.
2. Control—v. 16. We choose who controls our lives—Rom. 12:1-2. See also I Cor. 6:19.
3. Change—v. 17. Though formerly controlled by sin, through Christ we are now in the family of God—I John 3:2; Ps. 100.
4. Consecration—v. 18. The new life is Christ-controlled—II Cor. 5:17.
5. Complete—v. 19. "I speak with words easy to understand because your human thinking is weak. At one time you gave yourselves over to the power of sin. You kept on sinning all the more. Now give yourselves over to being right with God. Set yourself apart for God-like living and to do His work"—NLT.

B. The Choice of Separation—vv. 20-22
1. Problem—v. 20. If not in Christ, we are slaves to sin—John 8:44; I John 3:10. One remains a sinner by choice.
2. Pitfall—v. 21. What did sin produce? Shame and death—Gen. 3:10; Rom. 8:6.

3. Promise — v. 22. The results of being free from sin:
   a) Servants of God — John 1:12
   b) Fruit unto holiness — Heb. 12:14
   c) Everlasting life — John 11:25–26

C. The Choice of Salvation — v. 23
1. The pay of sin — v. 23a. Death — spiritual! Separation from God — Rev. 21:8. Unless man has his name in God's book (The Lamb's Book of Life), he cannot enter heaven — Rev. 21:27; 20:15. We reap what we sow — Gal. 6:7–8.
2. Promise of salvation — v. 23b. God's gift is eternal life; God loved us and gave His Son — John 3:16. Salvation is the gift of God — Eph. 2:8–9.

After one accepts Christ, choices remain to be made daily. Paul said we must work out our own salvation — Phil. 2:12. We must decide to attend church, read God's Word, pray and follow the teachings of Christ — John 14:15. Life or death lies within the power of our choice.

12 The Weakness of the Law

Romans 7:1–13

The Old Testament law didn't save man from his sin — it only revealed his sins. Christ came to save man and to reinstate him. He is the way to the Father — John 14:6. Several times He said, "Ye have read...but I say unto you." The Old Testament law was an eye for an eye. Christ said, "turn the cheek," "love your enemies."

A. The Comparison — vv. 1–3
1. Control — v. 1. The Jewish law controls man as long as he lives. See Gal. 3:23–25. Faith removes our connection to the law.
2. Comparison — vv. 2–3
   a) Sacredness of marriage — v. 2. The wife is bound to the

husband. Only if the husband dies is she free to remarry.
  b) Sin—v. 3. The sinner is bound to the law, but Christ died to replace the law. Now we are free to follow Him.

B. The Control—vv. 4-6
  1. Dead—v. 4. "My Christian brothers, that is the way it is with you. You were under the power of the Jewish Law, but now you are dead to it because you are joined to another. You are joined to Christ who was raised from the dead. This is so we may be what God wants us to be. Our lives are to give fruit for Him"—NLT.
  2. Desires—v. 5. While in sin, we followed its desires—John 8:34.
  3. Deliverance—v. 6. We are no longer under the law when we are born again—John 3:1-8.

C. The Commandments—vv. 7-11
  1. The power—v. 7. The law revealed sin. God's law is perfect—Ps. 19:7; in Christ we are cleansed from all sin.
  2. Perception—vv. 8-9. "The Jewish Law made me to know how much I was sinning. It showed me I had a desire for all kind of things. For without the Law, sin is dead. I was once alive. That was when I did not know what the Law said I had to do. Then I found that I had broken the Law. I knew I was a sinner. Death was mine because of the Law"—NLT.
  3. The problem—vv. 10-11. Only Christ could promise and give life—Acts 4:12; John 14:6.

D. The Consequences—vv. 12-13
  1. Holy commandments—v. 12. The Scriptures are given for our reproof, correction and instruction in righteousness—II Tim. 3:16. The Jewish ceremonial laws were for a limited time.
  2. Helpless commandments—v. 13. The law was not wrong—it just gave man a picture of his sin and its consequences.

Man is not saved by good works, nor by keeping any law, but by grace—Eph. 2:8-9. The Rich Young Ruler kept the law, but he did not have eternal life—Mark 10:17-22. Jesus said to Nicodemus (a religious man), "Ye must be born again"—John 3:3. Self-righteousness will not suffice; we must come to God His way.

13 Servants of God or Sin

Romans 7:14–25

Sin and Satan are powerful forces to be dealt with. There will always be temptation. All men's problems could be traced to three powers: (1) sin, (2) self, (3) Satan. Only as we overcome these can we experience the victorious Christian life.

A. Slavery to Sin — vv. 14–17
1. Control — v. 14. "We know that the Jewish Law is right and good, but I am a person who does what is wrong and bad. I am not my own boss. Sin is my boss" — NLT.
2. Confusion — v. 15. Will-power, determination and resolutions are not enough! Christ must change the life.
3. Complaint — vv. 16–17. "When I do the thing I do not want to do, it shows me that the Law is right and good. So I am not doing it. Sin living in me is doing it" — NLT.

B. Servant to Sin — vv. 18–20
1. Self — v. 18. In the flesh is no good thing. In ourselves we can do nothing — John 15:5. We must abide in Christ.
2. Sufficiency — v. 19. "When I want to do good, I don't; and when I try not to do wrong, I do it anyway" — LB. In ourselves we are weak; our sufficiency is in God — II Cor. 3:5; John 3:27.
3. Sin — v. 20. We must control sin, or sin will control us. Christ gives us strength to overcome and be victorious in all things — Phil. 4:13; I John 4:4.

C. Salvation from Sin — vv. 21–25
1. Desire — v. 21. Although we desire to do good, without God's help we practice evil. The heart is evil — Jer. 17:9. Out of the heart man acts — Matt. 15:19.
2. Delight — v. 22. Delight in God's law is the new nature at work. Blessed are the pure in heart — Matt. 5:8.
3. Destruction — v. 23. Sin wars against the good desires of the heart. We are in a battle — Eph. 6:12; I Peter 5:8.

4. Deliverance—vv. 24-25
   a) Failure—v. 24. Struggling, despairing, we need deliverance!
   b) Freedom—v. 25. Freedom over the power of sin comes through Jesus Christ alone.

Thank God, we can be the victors through Jesus. We have a choice. Under the control of God, we have victory over sin, the world, flesh and the devil.

14 The Power of the Spirit

Romans 8:1-19

The Holy Spirit is the third member of the Trinity. Jesus describes the person and work of the Holy Spirit in John 16. We may be taught lessons not learned from books or man if we allow the Holy Spirit to work in us.

A. Freedom Through the Spirit—vv. 1-4
1. Contentment—v. 1. No condemnation in Christ—John 3:18.
2. Christ—v. 2. The power of the life-giving Spirit is ours through Christ—John 5:24.
3. Commandments—v. 3. What the law could not do for man, God gave His Son to accomplish—Heb. 7:19.
4. Conversion—v. 4. "So now we can obey God's laws if we follow after the Holy Spirit and no longer obey the old evil nature within us"—LB.

B. Failure Without the Spirit—vv. 5-8
1. Comparison—v. 5. Those who follow the flesh will practice sinful living—Gal. 5:19-21. Spiritual fruit is seen in Galatians 5:22-23.
2. Choice—v. 6. We have a choice—"to be carnally-minded is death but to be spiritually-minded is life and peace." See also Rom 6:23; John 10:10; Phil. 4:7.

3. Corruption—vv. 7-8. Carnal living cannot please God—Rom. 1:28; I Cor. 6:9-10.

C. Faith Through the Spirit—vv. 9-11
1. Salvation—v. 9. "But you are not doing what your sinful old selves want to do. You are doing what the Holy Spirit tells you to do, if you have God's Spirit living in you. No one belongs to Christ if he does not have Christ's Spirit in him"—NLT.
2. Submission—v. 10. When Christ is in us, our body is dead to sin; we have crucified the flesh, affections and lusts—Gal. 2:20; 5:24.
3. Spirit—v. 11. The Holy Spirit will quicken our mortal bodies as it quickened the body of Christ—John 6:63.

D. Fellowship Through the Spirit—vv. 12-19
1. Spirit led—vv. 12-15. We are not to live the old way after we have been born again—John 3:1-8. We are then sons of God—John 1:12. We have been adopted into God's family—Gal. 4:5-6.
2. Spiritual liberty—vv. 16-17. We no longer are in bondage. God's Spirit in us is the proof that we are His children and heirs—Titus 3:7.
3. Spiritual longing—vv. 18-19. Present sufferings are not worthy to be compared with the glories of heaven—II Cor. 4:17. We desire to be with Christ.

If we permit, the Holy Spirit will guide, teach and make us what God wants us to be; but we must be willing to cooperate. Certain things we must do ourselves, but the Spirit will work in us and through us, if we permit Him to do so.

15 The Assurance of Salvation

Romans 8:20-34

God's promises are true. He cannot lie — Num. 23:19. What He promised, He will do. He will save all who call on His name — Rom. 10:13. Jesus didn't die for a select few — He died for all. It is not God's will that any perish, but that all be saved — II Peter 3:9. He will forgive all sin if we confess to Him — I John 1:9.

A. Promised Freedom -- vv. 20-23
  1. Promise — vv. 20-21. "For on that day thorns and thistles, sin, and death, and decay — the things that overcame the world against its will at God's command — will disappear, and the world around us will share in the glorious freedom from sin which God's children enjoy" — LB.
  2. Pleasure — v. 23. God's children look forward to being with Him. See Heb. 11:10.

B. Promised Forgiveness — vv. 24-27
  1. Salvation — vv. 24-25. Salvation by hope. Our faith is in this hope of I John 3:2. See also I Peter 3:15.
  2. Spirit — v. 26. Intercession in prayer for others — James 5:16. The Spirit can take control of us and pray through us.
  3. Supernatural — v. 27. "God knows the hearts of men. He knows what the Holy Spirit is thinking. The Holy Spirit prays for those who belong to Christ the way God wants Him to pray" — NLT.

C. Promised Faithfulness — vv. 28-30
  1. Divinity — v. 28. God uses everything in our lives for His glory, even our failures and mistakes. See Gen. 45:5. Job knew God had a purpose in all his losses — Job 19:25.
  2. Design — vv. 29-30. God knows who will be saved. He gives man a choice; He wants us to be like His Son. Cf. II Cor. 3:18.

D. Promised Fellowship — vv. 31–34

    1. Protection — v. 31. If God is on our side it doesn't matter who is against us. No one can destroy our character except ourselves. See Isa. 54:17. Gossip, lying and criticism against God's child may for the moment seem to destroy; but God will use this for good.

    2. Promise — v. 32. God gave us His Son. He will give us all we need — Phil. 4:19. There is a difference between our need and our greed! — Ps. 37:25.

    3. Pardon — vv. 33–34. Who can criticize those whom God has justified? To them there is no condemnation — Rom. 8:1; Ps. 103:3.

The Bible says that *whosoever* will call on the name of the Lord will be saved — Rom. 10:13; *whosoever* believes in Him will have everlasting life — John 3:16. He rejects none who come to Him — John 6:37.

16 Untouchable in Christ

Romans 8:35–39

We must be "in Christ" for divine protection — II Cor. 5:17. See also Ps. 91. If we stray, God will not force His care on us.

A. The Seeking — v. 35

    1. Seeking — v. 35a. What will separate us from Christ? Hebrews 3:12, "departing from the living God," is an admonishment to Christians. One can take an indifferent attitude to God and be separated from Him.

    2. Separation — v. 35b. Will we permit these things to separate us from Christ?

        a) Tribulation (trouble). See Rom. 5:3–4.

        b) Distress. We can have peace in Him — Phil. 4:7.

        c) Persecution (mistreatment for Christ's sake). See II Tim. 3:12.

d) Famine. See Ps. 37:25.

e) Naked. See Phil. 4:19.

f) Peril or sword (threatened by death). See Matt. 24:9. Paul said nothing would move him—Acts 20:24. He allowed nothing to discourage him from serving Christ.

B. The Scriptures—vv. 36-37

1. Prophecy—v. 36. "No, for the Scriptures tell us that for His sake we must be ready to face death at every moment of the day—we are like sheep awaiting slaughter"—LB. "Our adversary, the devil, walks about like a roaring lion, seeking whom he may devour"—I Peter 5:8.

2. Power—v. 37. In Him we are conquerors.

a) Power—John 16:33. Christ overcame the world.

b) Practice—Rev. 12:11. We can overcome by the blood of the Lamb and the word of our testimony.

c) Plan—I John 5:4. If we are born of God, we will overcome the world.

d) Promise—Rev. 3:21. Overcomers will live with Him. We can be conquerors through the power He gives us—Phil. 4:13.

C. The Security—vv. 38-39

1. Persuaded—vv. 38-39a. "For I am convinced that nothing can ever separate us from his love. Death can't, and life can't. The angels won't, and all the powers of hell itself cannot keep God's love away. Our fears for today, our worries about tomorrow, or where we are, high above the sky, or in the deepest ocean"—LB. He will not forsake us—Matt. 28:20; Heb. 13:5.

2. Provision—v. 39b. "Nothing will ever be able to separate us from the love of God demonstrated by our Lord Jesus Christ when He died for us"—LB.

We have freedom of choice; we may remain in Christ, or we may stray and backslide. Note the importance of abiding under the shadow of the Almighty—Ps. 91. No one can remove us from God's hand, but we can remove ourselves by choice. Note that Hebrews 6:4-6 was written to Christians.

17 The Plan of God

Romans 9:1–18

God's plan and purpose are revealed in the Old Testament. Christ would come through the Jewish race. (See the genealogy of Christ in Matthew 1:1–17.) God's ways are above our ways, but some day we will understand His perfect will. We know God's way is best for us.

A. The People of God — vv. 1–5
1. Concern — vv. 1–2. Paul had a great sorrow for the Jews. Christ had this same sorrow — Luke 13:34. His heart was broken as He wept over the city — Luke 19:41.
2. Compassion — v. 3. Paul was willing to lose his salvation if it would save his people. Cf. Exod. 32:32; Matt. 9:36.
3. Chosen — v. 4. "They are Jews and are the people God chose for Himself. He shared His shining greatness with them and gave them His Law and a way to worship. They have His promises" — NLT.
4. Christ — v. 5. Great spiritual leaders were forefathers of these Jewish people. Christ was of Jewish descent — Matt. 1:1; Isa. 7:14; 9:6.

B. The Promises of God — vv. 6–13
1. Plan — v. 6. Not all Jews have a part in God's plan and promises.
2. Promise — vv. 7–8. "Not all of Abraham's family are children of God. God told Abraham, 'Only the family of Isaac will be called your family' (Gen. 21:9–12). This means that children born to Abraham are not all children of God. Only those that are born because of God's promise to Abraham are His children" — NLT.
3. Prophecy — vv. 9–13
   a) Supernatural — v. 9. The prophecy of a son to Abraham and Sarah was fulfilled as God promised — Gen. 18:10.
   b) Scripture — vv. 10–11. Rebecca had two sons (Esau and

Jacob). God knew what kind of men they would be before they were born.

c) Service — vv. 12-13. The elder would serve the younger — Gen. 25:23; Mal. 1:2, 13. Jacob represents God's chosen people. Esau represents those not serving God.

C. The Plan of God — vv. 14-18

1. Purity — v. 14. Is God unfair? Of course not! He is righteous in all His dealings — Ps. 119:137.
2. Purpose — v. 15. "I will have lovingkindness and loving-pity for anyone I want to" (Exod. 33:19; NLT).
3. Personality — v. 16. God gives gifts or chooses people according to His foreknowledge and the yielding of the person.
4. Plan — v. 17. God used Pharaoh to carry out His work — Exod. 9:16.
5. Pleasure — v. 18. God's will is above our understanding — Isa. 55:8.

The Christian life is a life of faith. We may not understand. We may question. But we must trust His Word, will and way. Great men of God were great because of their faith — Heb. 11. They didn't understand, but they obeyed. God's plan is best for you. Let Him work in your life.

30

18 Acceptance or Rejection

Romans 9:19–33

Christ came to His own people and they rejected Him—John 1:11. The gospel was first preached to the Jew, then to the Gentile; it is for all who believe. Those who accept are God's sons—John 1:12; I John 3:2.

A. The Perfecting—vv. 19–24

1. Complaint—v. 19. "Well then, why does God blame them for not listening? Haven't they done what He made them do?"—LB.
2. Cooperation—vv. 20–21. The potter has power over the clay. We should be as clay in God's hands—Isa. 45:9; Jer. 18:6. Let Him make you what He wants you to be—Matt. 4:19.
3. Control—vv. 22–23. God wants us to bring honor and glory to Him. We will show forth His power. He will reveal His riches through us—Eph. 2:7.
4. Chosen—v. 24. He chose us, not only the Jews—Eph. 1:4; Rom. 1:16.

B. The Prophecy—vv. 25–29

1. Prophecy (from Hos. 2:23)—v. 25. In the family of God—John 1:12. Sons of God, to be with Him and be like Him—I John 3:2–3.
2. Pardon—v. 26. "And the heathen, of whom it was once said, 'You are not My people,' shall be called 'sons of the Living God' "—LB.
3. Prediction—vv. 27–28. Of many Jews, only a few would be saved. God will do as He promised—Isa. 10:22–23. Christ was rejected—Isa. 53:3; John 1:11.
4. Power—v. 28. God's power will execute righteous judgment. He keeps good records. Note Rev. 20:11–15, "The books will be opened."

C. The Problem — vv. 30-33

1. Pardon — v. 30. Salvation is offered to the Gentiles who were made righteous by accepting Christ — II Cor. 5:17. His blood cleanses from all sin — I John 1:7, 9.
2. Problem — vv. 31-32. The Jews didn't seek Christ for pardon. Depended on their good works and stumbled over the Rock, Christ Jesus — Acts 4:12; Eph. 2:8-9. It is through God's mercy that He saved us — Titus 3:5.
3. Prophecy (from Isa. 8:14; 28:16) — v. 33. "Those who believe in Him will never be disappointed" — LB. The builders rejected Christ.

Our eternal destiny depends on what we do with the gospel — Mark 16:16. If we accept, we are born again — John 3:1-8; we become children of God. If we reject, we remain children of the devil — John 8:44; we are already condemned — John 3:18. When we accept Christ, He changes us; daily He makes us what He wants us to be.

19 The Plan
of Salvation

Romans 10:1-21

What is salvation? It is more than baptism and church membership! There are many teachings about salvation, but Jesus is the only way — John 14:6. There is only one name whereby we may be saved — Acts 4:12. There is a way that seems right, but the end thereof is death — Prov. 14:12.

A. The Person — vv. 1-8

1. Wish — v. 1. Paul prays for Israel's salvation through their Messiah.
2. Wrong — vv. 2-3.
   a) Religious — v. 2. They had a form of religion, but no reality — II Tim. 3:5.

b) Righteousness — v. 3. The Jews were ignorant of God's righteousness, unwilling to accept God's way.
3. Way — vv. 4–8
a) Saviour — v. 4. Christ gives more than could be hoped for by those who trust only in the law.
b) Sinless — v. 5. If man were without sin, he would not need Christ — Rom. 3:23.
c) Salvation — vv. 6–8. Salvation is as near as belief and confession.

B. The Pattern — vv. 9–13
1. Confession — v. 9. Confess that Christ rose from the dead — I Cor. 15:13–22.
2. Conversion — v. 10. Believing in heart and mind means action; it means a changed life, a new heart — Ezek. 36:26.
3. Concept — vv. 11–12. We must understand that salvation is for all people.
4. Calling — v. 13. Calling on the name of the Lord and confession are closely linked — I John 1:9.

C. The Preaching — vv. 17–21
With salvation comes responsibility. "They" refers to the unconverted.
1. Problem — v. 14.
a) How shall they call on Him in whom they have not believed?
b) How shall they believe in Him whom they have not heard?
c) How shall they hear without a preacher?
2. People — v. 15. Those who preach should be supported by our prayers and our pocketbooks — I Cor. 9:14.
3. Prophecy — v. 16. See Isa. 53:1. Not all who hear will accept — John 1:11.
4. Practice — v. 17. Faith comes through God's Word — Heb. 11:6.
5. Plan — vv. 18–21. If any will seek the Lord, they will find Him — Jer. 29:13.

What are we saved from? (1) sin — II Cor. 5:17; (2) judgment — John 5:24; (3) Satan — I John 4:4. In Christ, we have power to overcome all temptation—I Cor. 10:13. Salvation is free, but it cost Christ His life. Salvation will cost us something also—Luke 9:23. Many don't want to pay the price—John 6:66.

20 God's Love for the Jews

Romans 11:1-24

The Jews play a very important part in Biblical history and in the future of God's plan. Through the years, many have sought, without success, to destroy the Jewish race. God's hand will remain on the Jewish race, fulfilling His plan.

A. The Review of the Jews in Scripture—vv. 1-10
1. Rejection—v. 1. Has God rejected the Jews? Though they have rejected Him (John 1:11), He has not rejected them.
2. Reception—vv. 2-4. Elijah felt alone. Yet there were 7,000 serving God—I Kings 19:10-18.
3. Reservation—vv. 5-6. Not all the Jews have forgotten God. He has a remnant. Note v. 6—saved by grace—Eph. 2:8-9.
4. Redemption—vv. 7-10. Some were saved.

B. The Rejection of the Jews in Scripture—vv. 11-12
1. Availability—v. 11. Salvation was available to the Jews, but they rejected it. Did God forget them? Of course not!
2. Accomplishment of salvation—v. 12. Though the Jews stumbled over salvation, through them others are blessed to accept Christ and become sons of God—John 1:12.

C. The Reasoning to the Gentiles in Scripture—vv. 13-16
1. Calling—v. 13. Paul's special call to the Gentile ministry did not exclude the Jews—Rom. 1:1.
2. Conversion—vv. 14-15. Paul desires that Jews and Gentiles alike would come to know Christ. When the Jews accept Christ they are like the dead coming to life—Rom. 1:16.
3. Comparison—v. 16. "If the first loaf is holy, all the bread is holy. If the root is holy, all the branches are holy"—NLT.

D. The Reception by the Jews in Scripture — vv. 17-24
1. Adopted — v. 17. "But some of the branches (who are the Jews) were broken off. You who are not Jews were put in the place where the branches had been broken off. Now you are sharing the rich root of the olive tree" — NLT.
2. Attitude — vv. 18-20. Gentiles are not more favored than the Jews. The Jews were the broken-off branches that rejected Christ. The Gentiles were grafted in.
3. Apostasy — vv. 21-22. If God spared not the natural branches (the Jews), will He spare the Gentiles who reject Him? See II Peter 2:4.
4. Accepted — vv. 23-24. If the Jews trust Christ, they will be reinstated in God's family — Rom. 10:13.

In the closing days of this age, more Jews are turning to Christ. In Revelation 14:1-3 we read that during the tribulation 144,000 will be saved — 12,000 from each of the 12 tribes of Israel. God loves the Jews and seeks to save them. All who call on the Lord will find salvation — Jer. 29:13.

21 The All-powerful God of Salvation

Romans 11:25-36

God is all-wise. He doesn't make mistakes. He is the Alpha and Omega — Rev. 1:8. He is eternal — Ps. 90:2. He had no beginning and He will have no ending. There is only one true God — Isa. 43:10-11. He knows the past as well as the future. He works all things together for our good — Rom. 8:28. Though many have rejected Him, He still loves and seeks to save.

A. The Prophecy of God — vv. 25-27
1. Problems — v. 25. Christ, a Jew, was rejected by the Jews — John 1:11; Luke 23:18. As we near the end of this age, man is becoming more hardened to Christ and spiritual things.
2. Prophecy — v. 26. (Quotation from Isa. 59:20-21.) Christ

would come to deliver man from his ungodliness. The promise was first given in Genesis 3:15. See also Isa. 7:14; 9:6.

3. Promise—v. 27. When Christ would come, He would deliver man from his sin—I John 1:9. This is a fulfillment of Isaiah 27:9.

B. The Promise of God—vv. 28-32

1. Promise—v. 28. The Jews fought the good news. Due to their rejection, the gospel was then preached to the Gentiles. Yet God loves the Jews because of His promises to Abraham, Isaac, and Jacob.
2. Personality—v. 29. "God does not change His mind when He chooses men and gives them His gifts"—NLT. God's Word and character remain the same—Heb. 13:8. God keeps His word. He will not change—Num. 23:19.
3. Promise—vv. 30-31. God's mercy is given to both Jew and Gentile.
4. Problem—v. 32. Though the Jews are now filled with unbelief, God still loves and has mercy toward them. See Gal. 3:22-23.

C. The Personality of God—vv. 33-36

1. Person—v. 33. His wisdom and knowledge are above our understanding (see Ps. 104:24; Rom. 8:28; Isa. 40:28).
2. Prophecy—vv. 34-35. Who knows the mind (plan) of God? See Isa. 40:13-14; Job 35:7; 41:11.
3. Power—v. 36. "Everything comes from Him. His power keeps all things together. All things are made for Him. May he be honored forever. Let it be so"—NLT. Remember, all things were made by Him—John 1:3.

Though God is all powerful, He will not force man against his will. God gives man the power of choice: to choose Christ and have life; to reject Christ and suffer loss—John 1:11-12. Jesus came and was rejected; but those who accept Him become sons of God—John 1:12. We shall see Him and be like Him—I John 3:2.

22 The Serving Christian

Romans 12:1-8

Christians are saved to serve. All Christians need to be involved in serving God. Some do become involved in His work, but only half-heartedly. See Eccles. 9:10. When one becomes involved in God's work, he has a great impact on others.

A. The Surrendered Christian — vv. 1-2
1. Call — "I beseech you." Paul pleads with them.
2. Consecration — "That ye present your bodies." Cf. I Cor. 6:19. Our bodies are temples of the Holy Ghost.
3. Charge — "A living sacrifice." Cf. Luke 9:23.
4. Challenge — "Holy, acceptable unto God." God not only requests holiness — He requires it! See Heb. 12:14.
5. Command — "Which is your reasonable service." We are required to surrender. Not a choice — a command!
6. Conforming — "And be not conformed to this world." Cf. II Cor. 6:17; I John 2:15-17; II Cor. 7:1.
7. Change — "But be ye transformed by the renewing of your mind." See Prov. 23:7; Ps. 19:14.
8. Complete — "That ye may prove what is that good and acceptable and perfect will of God." We need to seek God's will for our lives — Ps. 143:10; I John 2:17.

B. The Serving Christian — vv. 3-5
1. Personality — v. 3. "God has given me His loving favor. This helps me write these things to you. I ask each one of you not to think more of himself than he should think. Instead, think in the right way toward yourself by the faith God has given you" — NLT. We need confidence, but over-confidence causes problems.
2. Personalities — vv. 4-5. As the body has many parts, so the church, or body, has many parts, each important in God's work — I Cor. 12:12-21.
3. Practice — I Cor. 12:1-10. These are the 9 gifts of the Spirit — Eph. 4:11.

C. The Servant Christian — vv. 6-8

God chooses different people to do His work.

1. Preaching — v. 6. God has set ministers in the church, pastors, evangelists, missionaries — Eph. 4:11.
2. Teaching — v. 7. If our call is ministry, serve in that area; if a teacher, then teach — Matt. 28:19-20; II Tim. 2:15.
3. Speaking — v. 8. Four-fold: (1) if called to speak, be faithful. (2) sharing — if this is your ministry, then practice it. (3) leading — if gifted as a leader, then lead. (4) kindness — if blessed with kindness, share it.

Every child of God has a place in God's work. No one can do your job — you can't do anyone else's job. In God's work, no job is small. Some jobs may seem more important than others, but in the sight of God, all work is important. Every worker is important to His work. Be faithful where God has placed you. Use your talent for His honor and glory.

23 The Mature Christian

Romans 12:9-21

Christians need to grow and mature in the Lord — II Peter 3:18. There should be daily growth. Jesus said we should seek perfection — Matt. 5:48. A non-growing Christian will backslide. His carnal living will hurt God's work and will create problems in his own life as well as others.

A. The Christian's Practice — vv. 12-13

1. Patience — v. 12. Patience during tribulation will bring hope — I John 3:3. Patience also promotes continuance in prayer — James 5:16.
2. Practice — v. 13. "Share what you have with Christian brothers who are in need. Give meals and a place to stay to those who are in need of it" — NLT. Cf. I John 3:17.

B. The Christian's Patience—vv. 14-16

1. Persecution—v. 14. "If someone mistreats you because you are a Christian, don't curse him; pray that God will bless him"—NLT. See also II Tim. 3:12; Matt. 5:10-12.
2. Partners—v. 15. Ezekiel sat where the people sat—Ezek. 3:15. See, feel and understand people personally. Spend time with them, learn to sympathize.
3. Peace—v. 16. Be humble. Seek peace. Be agreeable if possible. Never seek to be great, or to be a "somebody." Jesus told us we must become as children—Matt. 18:4.

C. The Christian's Peace—vv. 17-18

1. Patience—v. 17. "When someone does something bad to you, do not pay him back with something bad. Try to do what all men know is right and good"—NLT. Jesus said we should turn the other cheek—Matt. 5:39. Jesus practiced this—Luke 23:1-21. He prayed even on the cross for his enemies—Luke 23:34.
2. Peace—v. 18. Be agreeable with others. Be kind and forgiving—Eph. 4:32. Read and practice—I Cor. 13. Be a peacemaker. Practice peace daily in your life.

D. The Christian's Person—vv. 19-21

1. Patience—v. 19. "Christian brothers, never pay back someone for bad he has done to you. Let the anger of God take care of the other person. The Holy Writings say, 'I will pay back to them what they should get, says the Lord' "—NLT.
2. Practice—v. 20. If your enemy is hungry, feed him—Prov. 25:21-22.
3. Power—v. 21. Don't let evil overcome you—you overcome evil! See Rev. 21:7.

The mature Christian is a happy person, a helpful person. The life of a mature Christian will leave a lasting impact on the non-Christian. To become mature requires the discipline of yielding our lives to God, His Spirit, His Word, His will.

24 Christian Righteousness

Romans 13:1-14

Righteousness is essential for every Christian. The word *righteousness* means right living, right with God and right with our fellowman. To be righteous, we must have the proper relationship with our Lord; we will resist sin and temptation. Our own righteousness does not please God; we must be clothed with His righteousness—John 3:1-8. We should have a holy life—Heb. 12:14; I Cor. 6:17; 7:1.

A. Christian Respect—vv. 1-7

1. Respectful living—vv. 1-2. Obeying rulers (higher powers) is our duty as Christians. Paul says we should not speak against rulers—Acts 23:5. Respect toward God should make us respectful toward other authority.
2. Right living—v. 3. If one lives right, he usually has no need to fear those in authority. If we live the way God wishes us to live, we need not fear Him—Rom. 8:1-2.
3. Reasonable living—v. 4. "The policeman is sent by God to help you. But if you are doing something wrong, of course you should be afraid, for he will have you punished. He is sent by God for that very purpose"—LB.
4. Responsible living—v. 5-7. We are responsible for obeying the laws of the country; responsible to God and to our fellowman. The first four commands of the Ten Commandments relate to God; the last six to our fellowman. See also James 4:17.

B. Christian Requirements—vv. 8-10

1. Responsibility—v. 8. "Pay all your debts except the debt of love for others—never finish paying that! For if you love them, you will be obeying all of God's laws, fulfilling all His requirements"—LB.
2. Respect—v. 9. All Ten Commandments (Exod. 20:1-17) are condensed into Matthew 22:37, 39. Love for God will cause

us to love others. People will know we are Christ's disciples if we have love for each other — John 15:12.

3. Results — v. 10. If we love people, we will not hurt them. See Gal. 5:14. By loving our neighbor as we love ourselves, we are fulfilling the Ten Commandments — James 2:8. We not only love our friends, we love our enemies.

C. Christian Righteousness — vv. 11-14

1. Awake — v. 11. We need to be awake spiritually, aware that our time is short. Some do not know Christ — I Cor. 15:34. Christ will give us light — Eph. 5:14.

2. Alert — v. 12. Time passes quickly — John 9:4. Christians are not in darkness — I Thess. 5:4. Put on the armor of God — Eph. 6:11.

3. Attitude — v. 13. "We must act all the time as if it were day. Keep away from wild parties and do not be drunk. Keep yourself free from sex sins and bad actions" — NLT.

4. Acceptance — v. 14. Don't follow lusts. See James 1:14-15. To live righteously, we must obey the rules of God — John 14:15. But we must also follow the rules of the nation. The only time we have a right to break a law is when it hinders us from serving God. If we reject man's laws, we bring reproach to Christ — Heb. 13:17.

25 Christian Consideration

Romans 14:1-23

Christians need each other. It is important for Christians to live in unity — Ps. 133:1-2. We will then be considerate of others. There are various churches and modes of worship. How they worship or which day they worship matters little as long as they worship God according to Scripture.

A. Patience and Consideration — vv. 1-4
1. Acceptance — vv. 1-2. Don't be critical of those weak in the faith — Rom. 15:1.
2. Affection — v. 3. Don't be critical of those who may not eat certain foods — I Cor. 9:22.
3. Attitude — v. 4. Let God be the judge — Matt. 7:1-5; James 4:12.

B. People and Consideration — vv. 5-9
1. Decision — vv. 5-6. It is not the day we worship, but the Lord we worship that is important. After Christ arose, most Christians kept Sunday as their day of worship — I Cor. 16:2. Sabbath keeping was for the Jews only.
2. Dedication — vv. 7-8. "We are not our own bosses to live or die as we ourselves might choose. Living or dying we follow the Lord. Either way we are his" — LB.
3. Dedication — v. 9. Christ died to be Lord of those who have died and those who are alive — John 11:25-26.

C. Problems and Consideration — vv. 10-12
1. Criticism — v. 10. Why judge others? We will be judged by God — II Tim. 4:1; Rom. 2:16.
2. Confession — v. 11. Every knee shall bow — Phil. 2:9-11. Bow willingly now or bow by force later.
3. Control — v. 12. We are responsible to God — I Peter 4:4-5; II Cor. 5:10. A book of remembrance is written — Mal. 3:16.

D. Practice of Consideration — vv. 13–23

1. Problem — v. 13. Live so no one will stumble over your faith — I John 2:10.
2. Persuaded — vv. 14–15. Eating meat is not wrong unless it causes others to stumble. Eating meat offered to idols — I Cor. 8:4–8.
3. Plan — v. 16. Refrain from eating or drinking anything that may bring criticism — I Cor. 9:27.
4. Practice — vv. 17–18. God's kingdom is not concerned with what we eat, but righteousness, peace and joy in the Holy Ghost.
5. Peace — vv. 19–20. Follow the things that bring peace. "All food is good to eat. But it is wrong to eat anything that will make someone fall into sin" — NLT.
6. Purity — vv. 21–22. Do nothing that opposes your conscience. Self-denial necessary — Luke 9:23. Crucify self daily — Gal. 5:24.
7. Peril — v. 23. Disobeying your conscience is sin — James 4:17.

No Christian is in any position to judge others. We would not only hurt those we judge, but hurt the work of God as well. Jesus called those who judged *hypocrites* — Matt. 7:5. Christians need to unite and work for God — not against each other and God's work.

26 Responsible to God's Will

Romans 15:1-21

Salvation brings responsibility. When we accept Christ as our Saviour, we also accept Him as Lord and Master. Some called Jesus *Lord*, but didn't obey Him — Luke 6:46. Paul strove to be fully obedient to God in all ways. When he met Christ, he immediately preached Christ — Acts 9:20. Paul said he was not disobedient to the heavenly vision — Acts 26:19. Paul practiced John 14:15.

A. Responsible Practice — vv. 1-6

1. Service — v. 1. Strong Christians are responsible for the weak — Gal. 6:1-2.
2. Sincere — v. 2. So live that you please your neighbor for his spiritual good. See Matt. 22:39.
3. Saviour — v. 3. Christ didn't live to please Himself — Ps. 69:9.
4. Sacred — v. 4. "Everything that was written in the Holy Writings long ago was written to teach us. By not giving up, God's Word gives us strength and hope" — NLT.
5. Strength — v. 5. Live in harmony with each other and be partakers of the divine nature — II Peter 1:4.
6. Spirituality — v. 6. Glorify God in unity. See Eph. 4:3; I Peter 3:8; Pentecost came to a spirit of unity — Acts 2:1-4.

B. Responsible Prophecy — vv. 7-13

1. Receiving people — v. 7. Accept others as Christ has accepted you — the Golden Rule, Matt. 7:12.
2. Receiving pardon — v. 8. "Christ came to help the Jews. This proved that God had told the truth to their early fathers. This proved that God would do what He promised" — NLT.
3. Rightful praise — vv. 9-12. Pardon for Jew and Gentile alike — Ps. 18:49; Deut. 32:43; Ps. 117:1; Isa. 11:10.
4. Rest in peace — v. 13. Our hope in God: (1) Be filled with joy — Ps. 16:11; (2) Be filled with peace — John 14:2; (3) Abound in hope — John 14:3.

C. Responsible Preaching — vv. 14-21
1. Persuaded — v. 14. Paul was convinced of their faith in God, knowing it would produce results.
2. Preaching — vv. 15-16. Paul writes boldly, exhorting them to be true Christians, to serve God and live holy lives — II Cor. 7:1.
3. Power — vv. 17-19. The Holy Spirit working through Paul gave him cause to glory in his work.
4. Prophecy — vv. 20-21. Paul desired to preach God's Word to those who had never heard — Mark 16:15.

Paul was faithful to God's call when He met Christ. He remained faithful until the end of his life — II Tim. 4:6-8. See also Rev. 2:10. He had marks on his body to show he suffered for the Lord — Gal. 6:17. He suffered because he was faithful and responsible.

27 Concern and Care

Romans 15:22-33

Paul had a deep concern for the Christians at Rome, a result of his consecration to God. He urged them to cooperate and pray for him. United prayer is a powerful force; prayer strengthens God's servants; it changes situations; it changes people; it brings miracles. We need more Christians who are concerned for God's work and His servants.

A. Concern — vv. 22-26
1. Preaching — v. 22. Paul was so busy preaching God's Word that he had no time to visit the Roman Christians. Paul said to the Corinthians, "Woe is unto me if I preach not the gospel" — I Cor. 9:16. This was Paul's one desire.
2. Plan — vv. 23-24. Paul plans now to visit these Roman Christians. Acts 27-28 tells of this journey. He longed to be with these people. Paul enjoyed Christian fellowship and loved the church — I Thess. 3:10.

3. Poverty—vv. 25-26. "But now I am going to Jerusalem to hand the Christians the gift of money. The churches in the countries of Macedonia and Greece have decided to give money to help some of the poor Christians in Jerusalem"—NLT.

B. Consecration—vv. 27-29
   1. Sharing—v. 27. "They wanted to do it. They should help them in this way because they owe so much to the Christians in Jerusalem. The Jews shared the Good News with the people who are not Jews. For this reason, they should share what they can with the Jews"—NLT. They were willing to share. See I John 3:17; note Eccles. 11:1.
   2. Service—v. 28. After Paul delivered the money to Jerusalem, he would return. Paul gave his life, time and service in helping others. He taught them to accept Christ and how to live the Christian life. See II Tim. 2:15.
   3. Surety—v. 29. Paul was sure God would bless him as he came to Rome. He had faith for the present and future—Heb. 11:6.

C. Cooperation—vv. 30-33
   1. Prayer—v. 30. He requests their prayers. We should pray for one another—James 5:16. There is power in united prayer—Matt. 18:19.
   2. Protection—v. 31. Paul seeks prayer for protection and acceptable service.
   3. Pleasure—v. 32. Prayer for God's will and protection would take Paul to Rome—Ps. 143:10; Rom. 12:1-2.
   4. Peace—v. 33. Paul prayed that the God of peace would be with his people. See Phil. 4:7.

As a Christian, are you concerned? Does your concern cause you to act? Does your consecration cause you to leave all and follow the Lord? As we draw near to Christ, we will share in His compassion for others.

28 Fellowship and Farewell

Romans 16:1-27

Paul was always careful to thank the many who helped him in his work for the Lord. All were important in God's work. He reminded them of his love and concern for their spiritual welfare, encouraged them to continue to live for God. Paul warned often of false religions and those who would lead astray.

A. Christian Friends — vv. 1-16
1. Service — vv. 1-2. Phebe, deaconess in the church at Cenchrea, assisted new converts and was hospitable.
2. Salutations — vv. 3-16. Paul greets the faithful Christian workers.

B. Christian Fellowship — vv. 17-20
1. Problem — v. 17. Watch for those causing divisions. Don't have fellowship with them — I Cor. 5:11; Eph. 5:11.
2. Practice — v. 18. Many are deceived by these false religious leaders who teach them only what they want to hear — II Tim. 4:4.
3. Pleasure — v. 19. "Everyone knows you have obeyed the teaching you received. I am happy with you because of this. But I want you to be wise about good things and pure about sinful things" — NLT.
4. Promise — v. 20. Christ came to destroy Satan and his works — I John 3:8. "Greater is he that is in you, than he that is in the world" — I John 4:4.

C. Christian Favor — vv. 21-24
1. People — vv. 21-23. Timotheus — Timothy; Lucius — either the one mentioned in Acts 13:1 or Dr. Luke who wrote Acts and Luke; Jason — unknown unless referred to in Acts 17:5; Sosipater — Acts 20:4; Tertius — writer for Paul; Gaius — I Cor. 1:14. Erastus — II Tim. 4:20; Quartus — only mentioned here.

2. Prayer—v. 24. "May you have loving-favor from our Lord Jesus Christ. Let it be so"—NLT.

D. Christian Farewell—vv. 25-27
1. Strength—vv. 25-26. God will strengthen and establish the church by the gospel—Rom. 1:16; preaching—Mark 16:15; Scripture—II Tim. 4:2.
2. Supernatural—v. 27. "May God, Who only is wise, be honored forever through our Lord Jesus Christ. Let it be so"—NLT.

All Christians should help and encourage other Christians. This involves warning them of the false religions that can lead them astray. Always thank those who have helped you. Appreciation strengthens Christian relationships and encourages further endeavor for the Lord.